GRANDPA'S NOTES

60 Years of Grandpa Chuck's Notes and Tips on New
Possibilities, Opportunities, Dreams, Families, Athletics,
Coaching, and Business for Baby Boomers to Gen Z'ers

CHUCK COTTON

GRANDPA'S NOTES
60 YEARS OF GRANDPA CHUCK'S NOTES AND TIPS ON NEW POSSIBILITIES, OPPORTUNITIES, DREAMS, FAMILIES, ATHLETICS, COACHING, AND BUSINESS FOR BABY BOOMERS TO GEN Z'ERS

Scripture quotations from the Holy Bible, King James Version (Authorized Version). First published in 1611. Quoted from the KJV Classic Reference Bible.

iUniverse books may be ordered through booksellers or by contacting:

iUniverse
1663 Liberty Drive
Bloomington, IN 47403
www.iuniverse.com
1-800-Authors (1-800-288-4677)

ISBN: 978-1-5320-6144-8 (sc)
ISBN: 978-1-5320-6145-5 (hc)
ISBN: 978-1-5320-6143-1 (e)

Library of Congress Control Number: 2018913286

Print information available on the last page.

iUniverse rev. date: 11/07/2018

I, Grandpa, Chucky C. (so affectionately called by my six beloved grandchildren), dedicate this book to each grandchild:

Aidan Phillips O'Hara

Andrew Joseph Obriotti III

Jack Charles Obriotti

Stella Jane O'Hara

Smith Patrick O'Hara

Kathryn Jane Obriotti

Proverbs 17:20 says, "Children's children are the crown of old men; and the glory of children are their fathers." My beloved two daughters, Stephanie Jane O'Hara and Melanie Kathryn Obriotti, the mothers of my six grandchildren, were raised right by Joan Carol Smith, my beloved wife of fifty-three years, and me. These women are my heartbeat and pulse.

Now, proudly, Stephanie Jane and Dirk O'Hara and Melanie and Andrew Obriotti are raising their children the same way. Joan and I are so richly blessed with our six grandchildren. We thank our Lord, Jesus Christ, Son of God.

The knowledge and wisdom of all my life experiences are priceless and so relevant to my grandchildren and family and everyone else.

CONTENTS

INTRODUCTION

It would be nice to live our lives over, but we can't. However, my experiences and philosophies can be shared to help others do better in their earthly lives and prepare them for eternity. I feel God gave me a gift that I have to share with others.

Grandpa's Notes is my personal collection of the three-by-five note cards I have written since my youth. I usually carry blank three-by-five cards and pens to note and record a wide range of subject matter.

I was born in Oak Park, Illinois, in November 1943 to wonderful parents, Paul and Kathryn Cotton, graduates of the University of Illinois School of Music. My father taught music at La Grange High School. Because of a medical condition, he was rejected from military service but worked the second shift in a Chicago bomb factory while Kathryn raised me. After the war, they moved to Ridgway, a small village in southern Illinois, and both began teaching band and chorus throughout the school system. Ridgway was my mother's hometown and was an ideal town to raise children. The past three generations of her Phillips family had lived there.

The family were Christians and founded the local Presbyterian church. I became a member at twelve years of age.

My parents taught me, Charles Phillips, and my sister, Nancy Kathryn, the right things to do and to be good Christians. We are grateful they gave each of us a well-balanced childhood. Sometimes, though, we did not do the right things and sinned, but we always asked Jesus to forgive us of the sins we committed.

My athletic career in basketball and baseball was quite noted for a kid from a small town. My father and Bob Dallas, the coach, molded me in so many ways to become successful in whatever I did. Some of their lifetime lessons will be shared throughout this book and apply to anyone from any walk of life.

There is not another human being on earth like you. God created you to develop your soul here on earth to your fullest potential and do his will on earth as you will in heaven when you join him for eternity. Remember this: Your soul never dies; your earthly body does. *Grandpa's Notes* will help you to never gamble with your soul and to have a joyous earthly life.

1

I WANT YOU TO KNOW

Be full of life.

Live and work passionately.

Excel each day better than yesterday.

Take an extra chance.

Be all that you can be.

Ships do come in.

Forgive and forget.

Small victories are sweet.

Simple is best.

Fun is free.

Set yourself on fire.

There's plenty of room at the top but not enough to sit down.

Don't solve problems; anticipate them.

Mystique stimulates.

You are truly blessed and loved by Jesus Christ and God, who are one and our Savior.

"Even to your old age and gray hairs, I am he who will sustain you" (Isaiah 46:4).

If God brings it to you, he will bring you through it.

2 TIME-WORN TRUTHS

Listen first; speak last.

Effectiveness is a discipline. It can be learned and must be earned.

Buy more time; there is no cost.

Live each day to its fullest.

Give your time to others.

Anything is possible.

Get it right the first time. Soak it in; listen and comprehend.

Remember the triple-T process—*think things through.*

Respect the other person's time.

Don't be a know-it-all. Always learn from people with experience.

Why sleep extra hours that you don't need? It's a waste of time.

Treat yourself.

Make your home your castle.

Do not speak too soon. Work with your information, and ask as many questions as you can.

Never count your chickens before they hatch.

Take time to shine.

Imagination is one of your greatest assets.

Let your instincts lead you.

Do your work at 100 percent—*nothing halfway.*

Do not be the cause of your own problems.

Just be yourself.

Live where you work; work where you live.

Do it today.

Be prepared for bad breaks.

You can't control anyone but yourself.

Take advantage of every opportunity.

Enjoy life.

Experience all the good pleasures of life that you can.

Reality helps fulfill your dreams and always overrides fantasy.

3

MODUS OPERANDI

Get it done.

Fight back. Never give up. Underdogs face challenges, obstacles, and adversities with fiery energy.

Be very instinctive. Have an eagle eye.

Never have a day when you are not optimistic or enthusiastic.

Have a quick decision-making mind with quick thinking ability.

Prefer no meetings, only small-group or individual coaching.

Have zero tolerance for negligence.

Be a generalist with passion.

Stand tall and face up to your responsibilities.

Always present yourself professionally.

Have absolute control of your life.

Be courageous in your own convictions.

Do your best to make someone else's life better. Understand people.

Get to the point in the fewest words.

Know where you are going.

Respect everyone you meet. Greet people with a slight, warm smile; a firm handshake with a slight pump; and warm, genuine eye contact. Greet them with, "It's nice to meet you."

Polish your image, dress, personal hygiene, and mannerisms. Make yourself shine.

Respect your customer, the phone call, or the caller.

Always thank the customer for coming in or calling, and make him or her feel important.

Don't turn your back on anyone who asks you for help or those you perceive as needing help—*at least offer.*

Don't assume your success will last.

Success is greeting a new day. Greet God and Jesus Christ and say, "Good morning. I love you to absolute infinity. I'm your servant, and I'm ready to do your will today, whatever it is." Ask for strength, health, wisdom, energy, boldness, and guidance.

Thank the Lord for all the blessings given to you, and ask Jesus to forgive you of all your sins (because you've sinned and you're sorry).

Don't create work for others. Get it right the first time.

Be a good listener and don't interrupt. Soak it all in.

Don't depend on anyone but yourself.

Take care of your own business.

Recognize the rights of others, along with their desires.

Never speculate about other people or jump to a conclusion.

Iron out a mistake or misunderstanding as quickly as possible.

Commit your way to the Lord and he will crown your efforts with success. (Proverbs 16:3)

Don't let financial bondage rule your life.

See a problem for what it is; then dig into your creativity to solve it.

Feed off the news. Knowledge is profit. You first must be informationally rich.

You *must* be street savvy.

You can't make any money if your doors are closed.

Keep your team independent.

A true salesman must have the passion for the hunt, the shot, and the kill.

Take advantage of your mistake.

Keep your hard-earned dollars. Avoid a financial coma and life support.

Don't overpay. This rule is as simple as it is strict.

Live long and live well. Relaxation is where the money is.

Connections are power.

Turn opportunities into new business.

A strong strategy and high creativity are the keys to power marketing.

ZIP code marketing to the affluent is a must.

Make money for others. "Don't invest in me; invest with me."

Remember that your creditor is your best friend.

Cash will always be king. Pay credit cards in full; maintain good credit scores.

Buy long-term health care insurance, blue-chip stocks, and US Treasury bonds.

Do not buy depreciating assets, IPOs, or high-risk investments.

Hoard cash, gold, and silver in a secure lockbox. Don't let someone else hold it or give you a certificate. "You don't know what will happen in life."

Always keep your position where you can cash in. Remember my maxim: Ain't cash great?

Analyze the purchase. Ask yourself, "Do I really need it?"

Avoid impulsive spending. Step back and procrastinate over whether to make the purchase.

We are constantly selling something. Only four rules apply: (1) be excited, (2) sell yourself, (3) sell your product or service, and (4) ask for the order.

If you ask a premium price, then you have to give a premium product.

You never know what's around the corner.

If you don't know your future, at least know who holds your future.

Use creativity and think outside the box. It's an endless source of ingenuity.

Never fake a day of work.

Don't call in sick if you're not because you probably will get sick.

Investigate before you invest.

Don't start a fight. If attacked, however, use all-out legal guerilla warfare. Never, never let up.

Never sign for certified mail if you don't know who sent it.

Don't put anything in writing if you don't have to. Never volunteer information if you don't have to.

Don't ever give up your rights.

Don't be afraid to say no.

Use silence as a strategic weapon in deal making or decision making.

Test someone's anxiety level, and then follow up with their real interest levels.

Save money on attorney fees. Study our legal system as a lay person and represent yourself *pro se* (on your own behalf) until you need to bring in an attorney.

Incorporate yourself, form a trust, put your assets in the trust, and protect yourself and your assets.

Never divulge information to anyone unless compelled or force to do so. How do you know who you are talking to on the phone or meeting?

Always have your "war party" ready for battle, but first *always* ask your opponent, "Are we to bring peace pipes or tomahawks?"

Never speak to recorded calls, toll-free numbers, or foreign-speaking individuals; never speak to a stranger. Phone solicitors usually ask, "Is this [so-and-so]?" and then say, "This phone call may be recorded for quality assurance. Voice corruption then occurs, particularly if you say the word *yes*.

Avoid such words as yes and your ID. Never give out your personal data, such as address or social security number. The IRS and banks never use these tactics. Identity theft is worldwide, and you could get hacked and scammed.

Avoid links with your files and personal data.

Don't ever play hooky.

Don't cheat your employer by stealing time or money.

Always have pride in your performance.

4

WINNING ATTITUDES— BUSINESS AND ATHLETICS

There is a certain winner's attitude—a belief instilled in you—when you work hard, work smart, and work as a team. No opponent is unbeatable. This was part of my Illinois Hall of Fame coach Bob Dallas's legacy.

The following are some of my business/ coaching principles:

Winners must have a tremendous desire to excel. They must have the belief and desire to do something better than anyone else—to be the best who ever lived.

A good competitor never underestimates his opponent.

Give the game the best you have, and the best will come back to you.

Play hard, play tough, play rough, but play clean.

Keep on your toes, and you won't get caught flat-footed.

If a break goes against you, turn on the steam!

The super-pro is the one who can dig until he is dead tired, and then he can dig some more.

When you're through improving, you're through.

Why gripe? Fight!

The first rule of winning: Don't get beat; it's an awful feeling.

Your opponents are friendly. Let them help you.

Even an experienced competitor unwittingly will tell you about his bag of tricks.

At the highest level of competition, the champion has product sense and imagination and displays iron nerves.

Bold play is so vital that you might risk defeat in a do-or-die situation. The mark of an expert is the ability to search out the unusual strategy that will ensure winning.

The best never rest. Go full throttle

Keep the winners, and toss the losers immediately.

Winners usually profit from an opponent's error by pouncing like a cat on a mouse.

If you get beat, strike back quickly, and rough over the winner's exhilaration.

It's hard to lose if you keep a-comin' and a-comin' and a-comin'. *Never stop*—not even after victory!

5 DAILY CYCLES OF LIFE

From the war babies' generation to the Gen Zers' generation, cycles of life have not changed much.

Challenges prove, through cycles of life, that strong values are still needed today.

Do you know how lucky you are? You were created by God to live on his planet and then given the opportunity to live in America.

You were given a high standard of living— no hunger, little sickness, and all the pleasures of a democracy.

The power in your life is the Holy Ghost, who lives within you and prepares your soul for an eternal job for the Lord in his home called heaven. Know this: You will never die, and when your earthly body stops functioning, in the wink of an eye, you will appear in front of Jesus for an accounting of your life, as he is the only pathway to God and admittance to your eternal home that he has prepared for you. If you are not a Christian, however, and don't believe in the Crucifixion and resurrection and that Jesus is the Son of God, you will be cast into the darkness known as hell for eternity.

Make time to pray, and ask Jesus Christ to come into your heart. As soon as he does, you will know it and will repent all your sins and ask forgiveness. It is free. My Grandmother Phillips always said that greed and ingratitude were big sins. Sadly, today the greed of man is centermost in our society and the world.

Always give to those who cannot help themselves.

6

WHAT MAKES MY
BLOOD RUN HOT

- people with major egos

- unmotivated fat cats

- self-centered people

- greedy bureaucrats, politicians, government officials

- oath violators

- suckers

- snake-oil salesmen

- cutthroat pirates

- smokers

- druggies

- people with poor hygiene

- pretentious high rollers

- tacky and gaudy projects

- sinister, evil people

- fuzzy accounting

- irresponsible advertising

- hyped-up marketing

Self-proclaimed insolvency—analyze cash flow, income statements, cash deposits/withdrawals.

The acid test is always this: ratio of current assets to current liabilities on a current balance sheet.

If you believe it to be slippery, it probably is. There may be a haze around the situation. *Look through it.*

Violation of public trust is shameful.

Heartless corporations do not care. Trust no one. Keep your back to the wall. Don't be deceived. Such executives are uncaring bullies, callous and ice-cold.

If you have been conned, as a lot of snake oil is sold out there, rid the loss quickly, and then gain from the loss.

Beware the fake, canned- or forced-laughter individual.

Lending corruption—watch out for the sharks, usurious lending rates, corrupted loan documents, and violations of the RICO Act.

Figure the true cost of the money you are borrowing. The fixed amount, fixed payback time, and fixed payback amount will give you the true APR.

Lending scoundrels have many buzz words to deceive you.

Scummy media reporting "fake news" is horrific. Such major media broadcasters, reporters, and companies set examples for shady businessmen, companies, accountants, and attorneys who prey on you and will victimize you for their own gain. Such people are backstabbing partners, greedy entrepreneurs, crooked brokers, and shyster lawyers.

Don't let them get in your pocketbook. Control your own money.

Don't waste your hard-earned dollars on bad money.

7

WOULDA, SHOULDA, COULDA

Life in the fast lane is short. *Get out!* I did.

Life is just a mist in the wind—so short. The thought of eternity motivates us to do our best each day and not to sin. Do the Lord's will each day. This is true success.

I can't, but *Christ* can.

You must be highly motivated to try again when you have failed. If not, then back up and punt, and get out of the game.

Get in touch with your reality, and understand yourself.

Time races even more now. Live at full throttle!

Short on time, and so much to do!

Failure is usually caused by laziness.

I can't believe I did that. If you believe you can't do something, you're right. Believe you can.

Should and *ought* have no place in your thinking.

8

FILLED HOLES IN MY SOUL

For I know the plans I have for you ... plans to prosper you and not harm you, plans to give you hope and a future.

—Jeremiah 29:11

I have had a wide variety of experiences, successes, and failures in my seventy-five years, but the triumphs and the disappointments have filled the holes in my soul. We all face the bumps, potholes, and detours along the way. We have to figure out how to deal with these obstacles each day. The Lord is with us continually, but this challenge he presents to us is to gain hope and a glorious future.

My passion on earth was raising my two girls, Stephanie Jane and Melanie Kathryn. My reward was being able to walk Stephanie down the aisle. That was one of the greatest moments in my life. The other greatest moment was walking Melanie down the aisle. They were the rewards of fatherhood. My happiness and enjoyment was seeing the girls excel in their adult lives and through college. The key was my gradually stepping back and allowing them to make their own decisions early.

The Lord's blessings have richly continued, as I have six grandchildren—truly all miracles and gifts from God. I also add my sons-in-law, Dirk O'Hara and Andrew Obriotti, to the blessings from God in his bringing them to my girls as their husbands and as fathers in establishing their families.

My fifty-three-year marriage to my beloved Joan, my earthly rock, has completed the holes in my soul. I have been so richly blessed.

Stephanie and Melanie are their daddy's heart and provide the inspiration I need to complete my soul. Joan is my engine and the reality checkpoint needed to plug the holes in my soul.

As you go through *Grandpa's Notes*, share some of my notes with your family, friends, and acquaintances. The Holy Ghost is in your soul and guiding you, as Jeremiah 29:11 states.

GOOFY GOOFS

Straight Thinking vs. Goofy Thinking

You must have the ability to dance through the storm.

You have to learn how to kiss a sweet butt.

Renew yourself.

Restore yourself.

Reinvent yourself.

Have gratitude.

Never bet on a sure thing unless you can afford to lose.

Always bet on the jockey.

Have a cavalier spirit in the whirlwind of life.

Don't fear the dice roll.

Living on the edge isn't for everyone, but oh, the thrills for those who do.

If you hold bad debt, write it off, and concentrate on collectible debt.

Do as much living as you can.

Be thankful for what you have, and be thankful for what you don't have.

Put your hands together and make some noise. It's a big party out there.

I'm very good at what I do, so you do what you have to do.

Snuggle up happy as a cat, and follow the music. Enjoy your spouse.

If you're not willing to clean the johns, then you have no business being an entrepreneur.

You don't know what it is to have something until you lose it and have nothing.

If you can't do it right the first time, what makes think you can do it right the second time?

Don't confuse yourself on the what-ifs.

Don't fear adjusting your view when the horizon broadens.

I live for the moment, not the future.

The Bible does not guarantee the sun will come up tomorrow morning. I believe, however, the sun will come up tomorrow morning.

Dig in and expect a fast day.

Professionals find the cocktail corner where colleagues sip trendy cocktails.

Don't be afraid of risk as long as the risk is calculated.

10

DON'T END UP WITH INJURY OR ACCIDENTAL DEATH

Do not sacrifice safety for profit or savings.

Know with whom you are traveling.

Celebrate safely.

Hire certified limousine carriers when planning high-risk special occasions—proms, graduations, school parties, sixteenth and twenty-first birthdays, even the thirtieth or the Big Four-O parties.

Know the good places to go and where *not* to go.

Be cautious in the hot traffic zones at night.

Have the ability to spot avoidable errors.

Obey the laws.

The whiskey hit him about two in the morning. Don't drive.

Reduce your risk each time you can.

See dangers around you. Make your own choices.

Travel only if necessary.

Be happy you're alive at the end of the day.

Apply common sense and logic.

Fine tune your instincts, and let them guide you.

Live smart.

Know what's going on.

Don't do dumb things.

Stay alive.

The world lives with a constant apprehension of danger.

Never take a chance with your life. It is just plain stupid and not worth it.

Get together with friends, not strangers.

Don't trust a driverless algorithm.

Impatience is a road killer.

Avoid road rage.

Don't tailgate.

Don't speed.

Don't cut off other drivers.

Stay in your lane. Use the left lane only for passing.

Lose the distractions. Half of the incidents while driving are caused by distractions.

When approaching the traffic light, assume it is red.

Double-pump your head both ways before entering an intersection. Many accidents happen in intersections.

Drive with your palms down on the wheel at the ten o'clock and two o'clock or nine o'clock and three o'clock positions. Crisscross hands when turning the wheel.

Keep your eyes moving in short, medium, and long range, along with using side-mirror focal points.

Move your torso and head to check your blind spots when changing lanes.

Avoid texting and phoning when driving.

Don't fight sleepiness. Pull over and take a power nap.

Keep up with the flow of traffic.

Maintain your vehicle bumper to bumper, inside and out. Vehicle road-worthiness is a must.

May this book bring sound health to you and help you tune up your life.

TIPS

Eliminate obesity and stress.

Control sugar, salt, and starch in your diet.

Don't eat late-night meals, only low-calorie snacks.

Control how much processed food you eat.

Eat foods with soluble fiber and take a powder supplement of soluble fiber daily. (Buy a canister at Walgreen's.) Put two teaspoons daily in a bottle of water.

Drinks lots of bottles of water. Keep hydrated.

Eliminate sugar-sweetened and diet soft drinks.

Watch your alcohol intake. It's best if it's zero.

Do not smoke or use tobacco products.

Eliminate unnecessary prescription drugs.

Take a baby aspirin and a multivitamin daily.

Refrain from strenuous exercise as you age.

Schedule a physical exam every six months with your primary doctor.

I recommend that adults over forty have an endocrinologist conduct an extensive blood exam yearly. This establishes a baseline for the remainder of your life. It is a must for good long-term health maintenance.

Have eye exams and dilation yearly.

Keep your mind constantly active and maintain excellent mental health.

Viva la vida!

11

MAXIMS TAUGHT TO MY DAUGHTERS

Never, never use the Lord's name in vain—the Gd or JC word.

Refrain from all sacrilegious items, jokes, and communications.

Don't be indecisive. If you keep changing your mind, you'll get nothing accomplished.

Let go of wrong. Don't make a problem where there might not be one.

You're better off alone than in the wrong company, business or personal.

Don't be afraid to break the rules, as long as it is legal.

Be happy with the smaller things; dream for the bigger ones.

It is not worth a darn, it is not worth accomplishing, nor is it worth accomplishing if it is not worth a darn.

By asking questions, you understand someone else's wants.

Remember dead silence speaks as well.

Take heed of phony words such as *magical*, *breakthrough*, and *miracle cure*.

Don't allow yourself to be controlled by others. Gain strength and admiration.

Stand up and speak your mind, all with due respect to the listeners.

The first step always is to use logic and common sense, based on your knowledge of subject matter.

If it isn't logical, you probably have misinformation, so analyze who will benefit from it.

Successful people are those with the most information.

Always have consideration in your actions and decisions. Don't scar people for life.

Only rely on your best judgment.

Keep alert to each situation. Never underestimate the change in that situation, as uncertainty usually occurs and cannot be predicted.

Gain more knowledge, be informed, and know what is going on.

Have the ability to read between the lines when negotiating.

You must have a passion for the thrill of the hunt and then the kill when selling your product or service. Close and ask for the order.

Sometimes the best way to win is not to play.

Your passion and sensitivity make you a great listener.

Understand customer needs, fulfill them, and then close the deal.

Your self-esteem is reflected in your appearance. Always put your best foot forward when out in the field. Look like a winner.

Be smart.

Arrive early. Work late. Take short breaks. Rest your mind. Eat a quiet meal. Clean out the stress. Meditate. Burn the midnight oil. Read one chapter of your Bible daily.

Have the vision to see what you want to do instead of visualizing the wrong things.

Fine tune your instincts. Let your instincts guide you. Use your common sense and carefully consider your options.

Don't make knee-jerk decisions.

Explore new relaxation techniques. Don't let frustration get to you. Learn how to deal with Murphy's law, which states, "If anything can go wrong, it probably will." Short power naps are great.

Relax your body and mind, and stimulate your spirit each night before retiring by reading the Bible. Find total solitude and quietness, and turn off everything. Thank the Lord for the day and his blessings to you.

Use your innate strength and energy to clear out problems.

Don't take anyone or anything for granted.

Always keep your options open.

Remember what side your bread is buttered on.

Smile and have good humor.

Your smile makes you a sure winner.

Keep smiling.

Communicate with your smile.

Commit your life to preparing your children to live a better life than yours.

Love, time together, good communication, a healthy lifestyle, spiritual strength, and fun times are all integrated key points that help grow your children. Accept their individual uniqueness and encourage a positive outlook. Help them determine what their potential is, and help them to reach it.

Know when to let things happen and when to make them happen.

Ask the Lord each day to help you, and give yourself to him. Help others along the way.

Wait on the Lord for answers, solutions, and his help. He'll always be there for you. The Lord never fails us.

Live each day without fear or dread, both in your personal life and business life.

Be thankful first for the many blessings Jesus Christ gives you. That is *first*—have gratitude.

Deal with basics.

Always keep your position where you can cash in.

Know when to play dumb. It is a smart move sometimes.

Deal one-on-one with the decision maker.

Greet success with humility and respect. It can be taken away quickly.

Watch, listen, and learn.

Don't automatically believe something. Assume it is false unless there is absolute proof that it's true.

Don't be naive.

Mind your own business. Don't get into another's business.

Avoid sinful situations. We sin each day, but we *must* attempt to reduce our sins and ask forgiveness each night in our prayers to our Savior, Jesus Christ.

Run with the moment. Let your ideas flow, and jot them on a note card, as I do.

Understand others' limitations.

Many deals never materialize, and money disappears in the investment. Know what the hell you are doing, or don't do it.

Be sure you're right, and then go ahead.

Learn empathy by walking in another's shoes.

Don't regret growing older; it is a privilege denied to many.

Stand up and back your position with documented, proven facts.

Push for cash. It's always the best.

Get to the bottom of the problem quickly. Understand what needs to happen. Express your unique solution-finding abilities.

Togetherness works; networking works.

Networking expands your inner circle as well as your professional circles.

Networking gives you the ability to gain support of others. Networking is looking for opportunities to gain.

Personal integrity and your good name are your biggest assets.

Stick to the facts only, no fluff-type statements.

Double-check your sources when needed.

Networking allows you to feed each other information—friends, family, colleagues, acquaintances, and strangers who give you the support you need to succeed.

Networking makes initial contacts to stimulate your network.

Network with those from a variety of backgrounds. Listen and learn, as networking draws success.

In networking, you gain, publicly and professionally, as a leader in your career and your community.

Many of your networkers will tap in for your resourcefulness and assistance. Knowing how to source is the key.

Understand human actions—why people do the thing they do. Anticipate. You must have this key ability.

Listen to others brainstorm. Swap ideas, and eliminate those that don't interest you.

Keep going. Go on.

Chug, chug, chug ... puff, puff, puff ... ding-dong, ding-dong ... I *think* I can. I *think* I can. I *think* I can.

12
ATHLETIC AND COACHING PRINCIPLES

As a former coach and noted point guard and catcher in high school, my love of athletics has continued my entire life. I've been blessed to have studied the sports diligently and have appreciated and immensely enjoyed champion athletes and coaches for the last six decades.

I wish to share with you some of my athletic philosophies, which I have applied mainly to the various businesses I've had since I was thirteen years old.

Home plate—where every game begins and ends, where the catcher and the umpire play the game, where every run scores.

The leader, whether the catcher or the point guard, likes to have the ball in his or her hands.

Don't take your eyes off the ball and mess up the play.

Well-placed confidence in your signals is crucial for your team.

Ryne Duren of the Yankees was the most intimating pitcher of all time—he was a beast on the mound—thick glasses, scary-looking presence. He pitched a fastball at more than one hundred miles per hour, high and tight. He threw junk balls galore, spitters, knuckleballs, slow curves, and different speeds ... and never knew where the ball was going. Almost unhittable but got you out. "Stay alert" was his cry to the batter. (Talk about psyching out a batter.)

Expect a tough day every day.

Nolan Richardson's famous game of "forty minutes of hell" was my model in the 1980s. This coach disallowed even an inch on the court that was unearned.

Find the weakness; exploit it; make it weaker.

Do not foul and give them a free shot.

Free throws are free; provoke fouls from the opponent. Free points win games. Hit the free throw.

Take away opponents' free things (i.e., free throws). Don't foul. Seventy-five feet of court, bring the ball up uncontested, free, unguarded perimeter shots. Free time on offense, free time in the huddles—free time disruption overall. No turnovers as they get free possession. Do not foul and give them free shots.

Full court press—belly to belly—and holding their uniforms. Use a variety of presses with bench signal calling. Keep their offense off balance continuously.

Everyone on a team must be a starter. Rotate often with fresh legs to keep the "forty minutes of hell" going.

Defense is your offense.

Defense is by far the most difficult facet to master.

Defense shock is demanding. Act fast, react fast, adapt fast, and execute fast.

You must have stamina, tenacity, determination, and a diligent work ethic.

Condition, condition, and condition. Be better conditioned than your opponent.

You must be able to go full speed for the entire game, injury-free and sickness-free.

Good health and healthy eating and sleeping patterns are necessary.

Rest rewards come when you have done a good job.

A good defender knows when to try for the steal and when to wait patiently for opportunities he's bound to get.

Frustrate your opponent; create stumbling blocks.

Always work off an angle.

Never give your opponent a clear shot. Know where his sweet spot is. Disrupt him. Frustrate him.

Play one way until you're in control. Play hard. Coach hard. Discipline yourself and your team to focus on the win.

When you make a good play, don't let the rush of elation weaken your concentration.

When your opponent scores, quickly run the next play. *Don't* give him time to get his breath back.

Never overcelebrate.

Picking the right offense or defense is like choosing an entree from a menu. Just as it's hard to determine which delicacy will best satisfy your taste buds, it's difficult to figure out which strategy will work best. You must have many plays to win.

Always create a script for your strategy.

Seize your opportunities as quickly as possible; then take the lead. Force your opponent to play catch-up and shorten his strategy, to his detriment.

Don't give one inch of the court without a pressure defense. Offense starts with defense on the court. Successful rebounding requires a defender position. Most teams will shoot under 40 percent, so a lot of missed shots are available to be snagged. Spot each rebounder at a specific location and tell him after he achieves his position; then look up for the incoming shot. Position your front three and keep two back at half court. If your opponent breaks the defense for a fast break, don't worry about it because the percentage is with you.

Offensive strategies are always the key because the end result is scoring more points. The play away from the ball leads to scoring points. Don't focus on the three-point shot. The percentage is not there. The 15/20 ft game is the best. Ball movement without the ball—cuts, screens, pick 'n' rolls, back doors, open drive corridors, few passes, and focused on the stop 'n' pop. The shooter has a percentage shot.

A brash half-court offense with a needed bit of luck can often hoodwink your opponent with simple maneuvers and multidimensional tactics.

Part of the offense, of course, is the full-court press, whether a man-to-man, zone, trapping diamond, or box and one. (*Always* put your center on the player throwing in. Hands straight up. Block his vision.) Simple two- or three-man half-court offense's objective is the stop 'n' pop or the layout drawing, usually the foul (free). Master the head-fakes in the open court, such as go right, fake, get opponent to commit, then go left, which is what you wanted all along for the screen waiting for your short quick cut. Stop 'n' pop. *Swish.*

Most players do not know how to set a screen. Practice time on screens is as important as shooting free throws. Show me a good screening team with some stop 'n' pop shooters, and I'll show you a winner.

Game Preparation

Scouting reports are necessary, but don't change your game plan.

Psychological warfare begins before tip. Have the best-looking uniforms in the conference.

Eliminate long, baggy, ugly pants and jerseys that are too big or too tight. Have shorts that are trim-fit and three-quarters of an inch above the knee, sharp target socks, matching shoes, warm-up jackets that are lightweight, and a T-shirt warm-up underneath in the opposite color of the starters' jerseys.

Assistant coaches monitor warm-up time of the floor. When over, return to the dressing room for a grand entrance, ready to play, entering the gym just seven to eight minutes prior to the ref's whistle. The team is led by the head coach. Starters take off all warm-ups; second five leave T-shirt jerseys on.

Teams start running generic plays and then switch to defense and back to offense. By this time, they have broken a sweat and go directly to the center court for the tip. (No returning to the bench.) The opponents are mesmerized and come cold to the tip circle. The team is in gladiator-battle mode, and the forty minutes of hell start at the tip.

Second half starts up and repeats itself, regardless of the score.

Your team's image and reputation will psych out your opponents all year long. Nobody will want to play you. Remember to play hard, play tough, and play rough, but play clean.

14

DON'T GAMBLE WITH YOUR SOUL

Jesus Christ is your head coach, the ultimate decision maker for your soul—no one else, not even God, only Jesus Christ, the Son of God.

> For the Father judgeth no man,
> but hath committed all judgement
> unto the son. (John 5:22)

God is the owner of your soul, but he delegated Jesus Christ, his Son, to be the decision maker.

Your soul is all that matters—nothing else. On judgment day, we all will have to give an accounting of our lives—all the good and the bad. Only Jesus Christ can pass eternal judgment on us, the sinners.

John 3:16 guarantees eternity to those who believe that Jesus Christ is the Son of God. Those who don't believe are gambling with their souls and will not be admitted into heaven and eternal life with the Lord, God Almighty, and Jesus Christ, his Son.

I believe all people are equal under God's making and direction. If you recognize this and disregard one's color, origin, culture, or creed, then you will be treated and blessed as you want to be treated.

Acts 17:26 says God made of one blood all nations of men to dwell on the face of the earth.

All people have marked differences from one another, and you must respect those differences but may not necessarily agree.

Ask the Lord to help you accomplish his will and mission set forth for you. He never will fail you.

Trust others, that they too are believers in Jesus Christ and God. Recognize that they too are on a mission from our Lord, and help your fellow man to achieve his mission.

Only Jesus Christ, Son of God, can forgive you of your sins. His forgiveness is free. Just make time to pray, repent your sins to him, and ask for his forgiveness. If you don't, then you are gambling with your soul, and you will lose. Your lost soul will be bound for eternal hell—guaranteed!

The last of *Grandpa's Notes* is his encouragement to focus on the Bible. Make it your most prized possession, and study it daily. Go through the Bible, pinpoint God's works and Jesus's quotations, and believe them, regardless of who you are or what you have done. Be ready, and have your bags packed and a one-way ticket— no return, no cancellation, no refund—and prepare your soul for eternity. It's free.

Full throttle ahead.

Thank you for purchasing my book. I told you that you would love it.

—Chuck Cotton, a Christian, an American, and a grandpa